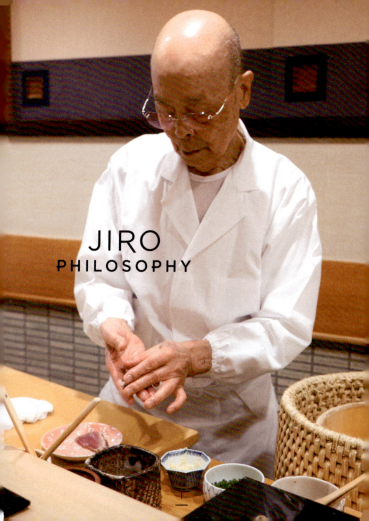

まえがき

　私は1925年生まれ、2015年の10月27日に90歳になりましたが、いまだに毎日お客様に鮨を握っております。

　8歳から料理旅館で働きはじめ、途中、第二次世界大戦がありましたが、職歴は80年を超えております。その間、一度たりとも、自分の仕事がいやになったり、仕事を休みたいと思ったことはありません。鮨職人になって、本当によかったと思っています。

　26歳のときに鮨屋へ修業に入りましたから、もう50年も鮨屋で働いているわけですが、いまだ鮨の仕事を極めたとは思っておりません。まだ、やるべきことがあるのではないかと、そのことばかり考えて仕事を続けております。

　90歳を機に「鮨」についての私の信条、流儀、心意気をまとめてみました。この一冊に、現在の『すきやばし次郎』の仕事が詰まっております。

小野二郎「すきやばし次郎」

Foreword

Born in 1925, I will turn 91 in October 2016. But I still make sushi and serve it to my customers. I began working at a restaurant-cum-inn when I was eight years old and at a sushi restaurant when I was 26. Apart from time in the military during World War II I have been working continuously in restaurants for more than 80 years. I have never once become frustrated with my work or wanted to take a break. I'm truly very happy that I became a sushi chef. Even after working at sushi restaurants for 50 years, I don't believe I've mastered sushi yet. Everyday, while working, I am constantly thinking there is much more to do. After turning 90, I decided to put my principles, style and philosophy into words. This book reveals all the work of Sukiyabashi Jiro.

Jiro Ono Sukiyabashi JIRO

2	**はじめに**　小野二郎	Forword
7	**Chapter 1**　小野二郎の言葉	WORDS OF JIRO
	Chapter 2　すきやばし次郎の仕事	WORKS OF JIRO
42	翌日の仕入れを決める …………	Deciding the Next Day's Supplies
43	築地最高のすし種 …………………	The Best of Tsukiji
44	次郎好みのまぐろ …………………	Jiro's *Maguro* Preferences
45	魚の素早い手当 ……………………	Handling Fish Quickly
46	食べ頃を見極める …………………	The Art of Timing
47	のりは毎日あぶる …………………	*Nori*, Toasted Daily
48	いい香りのわさび …………………	Aromatic Wasabi
49	たこは充分に揉む …………………	Massaging the Octopus
50	かつおは藁でいぶす …………	Skipjack Tuna Smoked over *Straw*
51	いくらも工夫の賜物 ………………	A Twist on Salmon Roe
52	江戸前のはまぐり …………………	Edo-style *Hamaguri* Clams
53	香り高いあわび ……………………	Fragrant Abalone
54	温かいえびの由来 …………………	Origin of Warmed Prawn
55	たまごを焼くまで10年 …………	Ten-year apprenticeship with Eggs
56	鮨の基本は酢めし …………	Vinegared Rice is at the Heart of Sushi
57	六本木店はより次郎らしく …………	Essence of Jiro in Roppongi
58	準備が95％ ……………………	It's Mostly in the Preparation
59	無言で進む仕事 ……………………	Working in Silence
60	にぎりは二人三脚 …………………	Working in Concert
61	握りも二郎流 ……………………	Jiro-style *Nigiri*
62	仕事道具を磨く ……………………	Polishing Work Tools
63	朝晩の掃除……………………………	Cleaning twice daily
64	**Chapter 3**　はじめに 山本益博	Introduction MASUHIRO YAMAMOTO

66	すきやばし次郎の旋律	Concerto of JIRO

67	**第1楽章　伝統** ……………………………………………	**TRADITION**
68	かれい ………………………………………………………………	Sole
69	すみいか ………………………………………………	Golden Cuttlefish
70	しまあじ ………………………………………………………	Yellow Jack
71	あかみ …………………………………………………	Lean Bluefin Tuna
72	ちゅうとろ ………………………………	Medium Fatty Bluefin Tuna
73	おおとろ ………………………………………	Fatty Bluefin Tuna
74	こはだ ………………………………………………………	Glizzard Shad
75	**第2楽章　四季** ………………………………	**THE FOUR SEASONS**
76	あわび ……………………………………………………………	Abalone
77	あじ ………………………………………	Japanese Horse Mackerel
78	くるまえび ………………………………	Japanese Tiger Prawn
79	とりがい …………………………………………………………	Cockle
80	かつお …………………………………………………	Skipjack Tuna
81	しゃこ ……………………………………………………	Mantis Shrimp
82	いわし …………………………………………………………………	Sardine
83	さより …………………………………………………………	Halfbeak
84	**第3楽章　進化** …………………………………………	**EVOLUTION**
85	うに ………………………………………………………	Sea Urchin
86	こばしら ……………………………………	Mactra Clam Muscle
87	いくら …………………………………………………………	Salmon Roe
88	あなご ……………………………………………………	Conger Eel
89	たまご ……………………………………………………	Grilled Eggs

90	**『すきやばし次郎』さんへ**	Homage to JIRO
	ジョエル・ロブション	Joel Robuchon
	マッシモ・ボットゥーラ	Massimo Bottura

92	**お知らせとご紹介**	Information and Profile

Chapter 1

小野二郎の言葉

教わったことをやるだけでは、
見習いと同じ。

" Just doing what you're taught is the same as being an apprentice. "

自分なりにちゃんと考えて味を仕上げていく。それから他の新しいものを作ってみる。そういうことを考えないと、いつまで経っても見習いのままだよ、と若い職人にはいつも言っています。独立したとしても見習いと変わりません。鮨を握るなんてことは、仕込みを覚えることに比べたら大したことはないんです。

I tell my young apprentices that they should think about how to achieve good flavor on their own, improve it and then experiment.
I always tell them if they don't they will be apprentices for life.
That said, once they've become independent they should still pursue improvement just like an apprentice. If you think about it, compared to learning preparation techniques, making sushi is not so difficult.

自分に合う仕事などありません。
仕事に自分を合わせるから上達するんです。

" There is no job suited to you;
You become suited to the job."

鮨屋のおしぼりってのは、とても大切だと思うんですね。にぎりは手でつまんで食べますから、おしぼりは清潔でないといけません。うちの店に入った若い者は、手を冷たくして手絞りします。まずこれをやらされます。コツがあって、一瞬にして絞ればやけどしない。これができないと魚に触ることもできません。

I believe that hot towels at sushi restaurants are very important. As customers eat sushi with a bare hand, the towels have to be clean. Apprentices here get their hands cold first and then squeeze hot towels while hot water runs through. That's their first job. Once you learn the ropes and do it quickly, you won't get burned. You won't be allowed to touch fish if you don't master it.

掃除がきちんとできなきゃ、
料理なんてできません。

" You cannot cook unless you can clean up properly."

汚れたらすぐに拭けばいいんです。時間が経ってしまうと洗わなければならない。一日経ってしまえば磨かなきゃならない。掃除の仕方を見るだけでも、料理に対する心がけが調理場に表れます。掃除はしすぎるということがありません。掃除がきちんとできなきゃ、料理なんてできない。それくらい大事なことです。

You just need to wipe up any mess immediately. Because if you leave it, you'll need to wash it. If you leave it for one day, you'll have to polish it. Your way of cleaning reflects your attitude for cuisine. You can never over-clean. If you cannot clean up properly, you cannot cook properly. That's how important cleaning is to sushi. is such an important thing to sushi.

準備に早すぎるということはありません。
いくらでも前からできます。

" It's never too early to prepare.
You can start preparation way in advance. "

できる限りいいものを仕入れるようにしていますが、台風が一番やっかいで、河岸に魚がまったくなくなってしまいます。うちは養殖も冷凍ものも使わないので、台風の情報にはいつも注意しています。ですから、準備はいくらでも前からできます。早すぎるってことはありません。

I try to get the best quality fish from the market, but typhoons are vexing as they prohibit us from getting ingredients. There are no fish is sold at the market after a typhoon. I don't use farmed or frozen seafood so I am always aware of meteorology and typhoon information. It's never too early to prepare.

手は、職人にとって最も大切な道具です。

" Hands are the most important tools for craftsmen."

にぎりずしは、職人が素手で握ったものをお客様が召し上がるので、手はとても大切です。年をとったときのことを考えて、40代から外出の時は必ず手袋をするようにしました。飯粒を触っただけで酢めしの状態がわからないといい握りができませんから、酢めしをつかむ左手の中指、薬指、小指の先はとりわけ敏感でなくてはなりません。

    Customers eat nigiri sushi that a chef has made with his bare hands. I started wearing gloves in my 40's when going outside. You need to keep the tips of your middle, third and little fingers on your left hand sensitive. To make a great nigiri sushi, you need to be able to tell the condition of the vinegar rice by merely touching it. In that sense, gloves are useful to protect my fingers.

当たり前のことをやり続ければ、
美味しくなるのは当たり前のこと。

" If you continue to do things the right way it's a given that your sushi will turn out delicious. "

仕事で特別なことをやろうとは思いません。ただ、面倒がらずに手間をかけます。人と違うことをしたいとかで根本から外れると、全く外れてしまいます。そうじゃなく、根本では、基本は同じでも、美味しく、美味しく、美味しくとやっていけば、いいものができると思うんですよね。

    I don't think I am doing anything out of the ordinary. But, I always devote ample time to my work. If you stray from the fundamentals—say, trying to set yourself apart from other chefs—you will completely stray off-track. I believe that by, adhering to the fundamentals and continuously striving to create delicious flavors, you will be able to innovate.

工夫には限界がありません。
誰もやってないことができたときが嬉しいんです。

" There is no limit to innovation. "

とことん納得のいくまで仕事を追求するのは、職人の意地みたいなもんです。どんなに手がかかることでも自分が納得できるまでは、人に任せず全部自分でやります。年をとっても面倒なことでも全部自分でやります。新しいことを自分で考えて、工夫してでき上がったときは、本当に気分がいいもんです。

Pursuing work to satisfaction is the pride of a craftsman. No matter how time-consuming, I will leave no tasks to others. I will do them all myself until I am satisfied. Even as I get older, I still do all the work, even if it's bothersome. I feel very pleased when I develop and create something from a new idea of my own.

お客さまのアドバイスは、
なるほど、と思ったら素直に受け入れます。

" I take customers' advice when it makes sense."

自分が正しいと思っても、そうじゃないことばかりです。大勢の人が相手の商売で自分の思いどおりにやって、それでみんなうまく事が運ぶなんてことはあるもんじゃない。いいアドバイスは受け入れて、それにいろいろ加味して自分の型を作るというのが大事な姿勢です。なるほど、と思ったら、素直に参考にする気持ちがないと進歩はないですよ。

Even if you think you are right that's often not the case. No matter what kind of business you are in if you only work in an inflexible way you won't find success. So, it's a very important policy of mine to always listen to my customers and take always their advice into consideration. If it makes sense then I will adopt it. If I don't, I will never evolve.

次郎では、面倒臭いは禁句。
手間をかけて美味しくするんです。

" Saying 'too troublesome' is forbidden at Jiro.
We invest time to create delicious flavors. "

仕事に打ち込んで仕事が好きな人は、楽しくてやりがいがあるから、自分のことで言うと、90歳になってもまだやりたいんですよ。だから手間をかけて美味しくすることを面倒臭いとは思いません。でも、誰にもわからないことをやるってのは、楽しいけれども、苦しいですね。ハッハッハ。

    People who love their work passionately want to continue working. I'm no exception. Although I'm 90 years old, I'd like to keep on going. That's why I don't find investing time in my work troublesome. However, while I enjoy trying to improve on flavor it is also hard work. Ha-ha.

先入観をはるかに超えてみんなが驚く
味になるまでは、何年でも試します。

" I will experiment for years to obtain a new flavor that completely transcends the ordinary. "

誰しも自分が知っているものにはイメージを持っています。その先入観を超えるには、何度でも何年でも自分の納得のいく味になるまで繰り返し試してみることです。次第に目指す味に近づいてきて、食べた人が驚くような美味しい仕上がりになります。そうなったら初めて、そのやりかたを若い職人に伝えることができます。

In order to transcend the ordinary, I will tirelessly experiment until I am satisfied with a new flavor, no matter how many times, or years, it takes. As I gradually get closer to what I'm pursuing, people who try my creation will express surprise at its flavor. Only when this occurs do I teach the method to my junior apprentices.

ネタが全部変わってきているから、これからの職人は、考えて味を上げないと。

" Since all sushi toppings are changing, sushi craftsmen must now factor this in when working out flavors."

海がどんどん変わっています。旬も、かつおなんて半年ずれてますから、そのときに旨いものを出さないといけません。昔の魚や貝はもっと旨かったから、昔の味を呼び起こそうと思ってもなかなかできない。昔のような味にしようかというこれからの職人は、ちゃんと考えて味を仕上げなきゃならないから大変です。

The oceans are quickly changing. For example, the season for katsuo (skipjack tuna) now starts six months later. But, we have to serve the best of what's in season. Fish and shellfish were tastier in the past and it is difficult to find their intense flavors. The next generation of sushi chefs will face challenges in trying to find ways to bring out and enhance fish flavors.

ある程度、腕が良くなければ、
それよりも上は目指せません。

" You've got to master some skills to reach the next stage. "

自分一人の力だけでは上へ行けません。だけど、ある程度の腕がなかったら、さらに上に行く助けを得られません。だから、あるレベルまではきちんと教わらなきゃならないんです。うちでおおよそ10年働いた職人なら、仕込みを一通り覚えて、独り立ちできるようになります。

You won't advance to the next level all on your own. You need to train properly up to a certain point. In the case of Jiro, after a decade of training a craftsman will have mastered everything from preparation to making sushi. He will be ready to strike out on his own.

鮨はご飯を食べていただく食事だから、
シャリが良くなきゃ美味しくありません。

*" Since rice is at the heart of sushi
if it is not well-prepared the sushi won't taste good. "*

みなさんネタのことばかりおっしゃいますが、もともと鮨はご飯を食べていただく食事です。だからどんなにネタが良くても、シャリが良くなきゃ握りは美味しくありません。あくまでネタは四分で酢めしが六分。その根本をおろそかにしてどんなに工夫を凝らしても、どこまでいっても外れたままです。

    Although most people talk about the toppings, sushi is fundamentally a rice dish. So even if the seafood is excellent, the sushi won't taste delicious unless the shari vinegar rice is perfect. The balance ratio is about 40 percent fish to 60 percent rice. So, if this tradition is ignored your sushi will miss the mark, no matter what you do.

職人は、自分がこさえたものを食べて
「旨いな」と思えないといけません。

" Craftsmen must judge their work to be delicious."

料理人はいつも美味しいものを食べたいと思う食いしん坊でなきゃなりません。私は自分で作ったものを食べてみて、旨いな、と自分でもそう思います。ああ、旨いなあ、というのは、普通より二重も三重も手をかけたから余計に旨くなる。いつも「これをもうちょっと美味しくできないだろうか」と考えています。

Chefs should be gluttons who are always pursuing the best flavors.
I try my own sushi and find it excellent. If I can qualify it to be excellent I have labored over the process two or three times more than usual. I am always considering ways to make improvements.

新しいものや考えを教わっても、
聞いただけでやらなければ何も変わりません。

" People will teach you new things and ideas.
But if you don't try them out you will not change."

自分でやってみなければ、どんなにいいことを教わっても、ただ知ってるだけで上達することはありません。仕事が本当に好きな人ってのは、自分のやったこと以上のものをどんどん考えていく。それが楽しい、そして自分のやりがいがある。そういうのが全部入っちゃうから、どうしても毎日何かやってしまいます。

No matter how good the teaching, unless you actually put it into practice, you won't be able to progress. You will only have the knowledge. People passionate about their work are always trying to improve on what they've made. It's enjoyable and rewarding.
Because of this, we can keep trying new things every day.

まだやれることがある、
と思う気持ちが大切です。

" Feeling you can still evolve is important."

もっと旨くするには、まだやれることがある、と思う気持ちが大事ですよね。絶対ありますよ、絶対ある、と私は思うよ。これで終わりと思うのはね、ま、死ぬときぐらいですよ。本当にそう思うもの。

It's important to have the feeling that there are still ways for making something taste better. I definitely believe so, definitely. The day I stop feeling that way will probably be when I am on my way out.
I am certain of that.

Chapter 2

すきやばし次郎の仕事

翌日の仕入れを決める
Deciding the Next Day's Supplies

仕事が終わってから親父さんと「明日はあの人が来るから、これを仕入れよう」「これを探してくれ」と考えるのが夜の日課です。こはだが好きな人がいらっしゃるときは余分に仕込んでおかなきゃいけない。また、同じレベルのネタを最後までそろえないと「おまかせ」の値打ちがなくなってしまいますから、仕入れが肝心です。(小野禎一)

    Every night, after work, our routine is to go over the plan for the following day—whether there is a regular customer with special preferences coming in or if there is a specific item my father wants me to source. If a guest is a fan of *kohada* (gizzard shad) then we must have a sufficient supply. We also have to assemble the same top quality of toppings for each entry in our tasting menu, otherwise the course loses its meaning. Procuring ingredients is crucial. (Yoshikazu Ono)

築地最高のすし種
The Best of Tsukiji

親父さんは、「いいものは高いのが当たり前」と、値段のことは一切言いません。コースの値段だけ決めて1年間の収支が成り立てばいい、という考え方ですから、常に最高のものを仕入れます。いくら値が張っても次郎は買ってくれるというので、仲買さんも常に最高のものを競り落とすことができるんです。(小野隆士)

My father says, "It's a given that fine things are expensive" and he never discusses pricing. As long as the fixed price menu balances out at the end of the fiscal year my father is fine. So, he is always securing premium ingredients. Since the suppliers know Jiro will pay for quality no matter how high the price they are able to successfully bid on his behalf. (Takashi Ono)

WORKS of JIRO

次郎好みのまぐろ
Jiro's Maguro Preferences

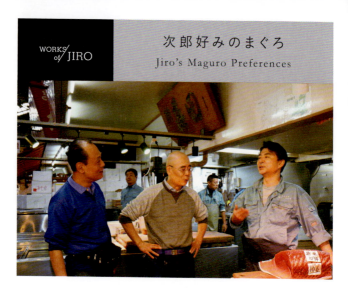

『フジタ水産』藤田さんとは、20年以上毎日のように築地で会っています。香りが高く味のキレがいい次郎好みのまぐろを仕入れてくれる藤田浩毅さんの他にも、次郎と取引している店は、次郎の仕事を信頼して協力してくれる専門店ばかり。信頼関係で結ばれた、なくてはならないパートナーです。(小野禎一)

I've been meeting Fujita Suisan's Hiroki Fujita nearly every morning at Tsukiji for more than 20 years. In addition to Fujita—who sources my father's preferred *maguro* (tuna), which is fragrant and sharp in flavor—Sukiyabashi Jiro has many other specialty suppliers who we depend on. These are indispensible partnerships built on mutual trust. (Yoshikazu Ono)

魚の素早い手当
Handling Fish Quickly

WORKS of JIRO

いい魚を河岸から仕入れてくるだけじゃいけません。あじやいわしは傷みやすいので、すぐに手当します。内臓を取ってよく洗い、適切な温度で保管します。いわしなどは握って3分で色が変わって美味しくなくなります。しんこの仕込みなんて本当に秒単位です。とにかく素早い手当が何より肝心です。(小野隆士)

Our work is not just about securing excellent fish from the market. Since *aji* (Japanese horse mackerel) and *iwashi* (sardine) spoil easily, they have to be handled immediately. We remove the innards, rinse thoroughly and store them at the correct temperature. Sardines, for instance, will change color within three minutes after being prepared as sushi, and will lose their flavor. *Shinko* (juvenile gizzard shad) is prepared in a matter of seconds. In any event, working quickly with fish is the most important point. (Takashi Ono)

食べ頃を見極める
The Art of Timing

まぐろなどは食べ頃を見計らって冷蔵庫に寝かせます。築地から買ってきてもすぐに使えるわけではないので、その食べ頃を見極めるのが私らの仕事なんです。さばも毎日3本ぐらい〆てから、冷蔵庫に寝かせて旨みが出るまで1週間ほど待ちます。〆足りなければ、ちょうどよくなるまでさらに寝かせ、そして朝晩味見をします。(小野禎一)

With *maguro* (tuna) and other fish, we must judge the optimum time for preparing as sushi and age the cuts, accordingly, in the refrigerator.

Since maguro cannot be used right after being delivered from Tsukiji, it's our job to determine the best timing for consumption. We also marinate around three saba (mackerel) in vinegar every day and age them in the refrigerator for around a week until the fish's rich umami is released. If we determine they're not quite ready we taste them morning and night until perfect. (Yoshikazu Ono)

WORKS of JIRO

のりは毎日あぶる

Nori, Toasted Daily

鮨屋がのりを自分の店で毎朝あぶって使うのは当たり前のことですが、今、これをやっている鮨屋はどれくらいあるでしょうか。梅雨時など、のりはしけってしまいますから１週間分まとめてあぶってもダメで、毎朝、紀州の備長炭であぶります。上手にあぶれば、夜になっても香りが立って、口の中ですぐに溶けてくれます。（小野禎一）

It's customary for sushi restaurants to toast their own *nori* everyday for their own use. Yet, I wonder how many are carrying on this practice today. During the rainy season, nori will become moist so toasting a week's worth is out of the question. At Sukiyabashi Jiro, we fan nori sheets over fine Kishu-binchotan charcoal from Wakayama every morning. If done properly, they are still aromatic by evening and will dissolve immediately in the mouth. (Yoshikazu Ono)

WORKS of JIRO

いい香りのわさび
Aromatic Wasabi

次郎で使っているわさびは赤い軸のもので、数も少なく値も張りますが、青軸とは味と香りが断然違います。それをゆっくりと大きな円を描くようにおろせば、やわらかな風味、豊かな甘みと香りのわさびになります。うちのおろしがねは真ん中が減って凹んでいますが、家庭で使ってこうなるには100年はかかるでしょう。（小野禎一）

At Sukiyabashi Jiro, we use *aka-jiku* (red-stemmed) wasabi, which is harder to come by and more expensive than the *aoi-jiku* (green-stemmed) variety, but smells and tastes a world apart. When grated slowly in large round circles the root releases a delicate flavor and takes on a pleasant elasticity.

Our graters have a worn indentation. It would take about a hundred years for an average household grater to take on this form. (Yoshikazu Ono)

たこは充分に揉む
Massaging the Octopus

たこを長い時間揉むというのは、親父が考えだしました。明石あたりのたこが、あれだけ香りがあって柔らかく旨くできるのはなぜかな、と最初はわからなかったようです。たこの季節は短いので、仕上げるのに３年ぐらいかかってます。今では充分に揉んで、より香りが立つようにほんのり温めてお出ししています。(小野禎一)

My father is the person who came up with the idea of massaging octopus over an extended period. At first, he didn't know how to prepare octopus from the Akashi area so that it would achieve its rich aroma and tender state. Since the season for octopus is so short it took three years for him to hit on this method. Nowadays, the flesh is kneaded for a long period and served at a slightly elevated temperature to release its aroma. (Yoshikazu Ono)

かつおは藁でいぶす
Skipjack Tuna Smoked over Straw

かつおは藁であぶると皮目に火が通り、香ばしさがつきます。ガスではなく藁の火でないといけません。親父さんが静岡の日本料理店にいたころ、職人さんがすずきを天竜川の茅であぶっていた。それを工夫して、かつおをすし種にしたそうです。この握りのためだけに毎年、無農薬の稲藁を確保しています。(小野隆士)

 By smoking *katsuo* (skipjack tuna) over straw only the skin is cooked, which imparts a fine aroma. Gas won't do the trick, only smoking over straw. When my father worked at the Japanese restaurant in Shizuoka, the craftsmen would smoke *suzuki* (Japanese sea bass) over reeds from the Tenryugawa River. He tweaked that method for our *katsuo*. In order to prepare this sushi, we store a supply of organic rice straw every year. (Takashi Ono)

WORKS of JIRO
いくらも工夫の賜物
A Twist on Salmon Roe

次郎のストッカーは、家庭の冷蔵庫では焼けてしまうものも新鮮なまま保存できます。あるとき、お客さまに美味しいいくらをいただいたんですが、旬は短く、いつも出せるわけではありません。親父さんが、魚卵のような生臭さがない卵かけごはんのような風味で冷凍して、一年中出せるようになりました。(小野隆士)

At Jiro, our refrigeration system can preserve fish, which would be burned in a home fridge in a fresh state. On one occasion a regular brought in a gift of premium *ikura* (salmon roe). Since its season is short it can't be served year-round. My father invented a way to freeze ikura so that its flavor has no fish egg odor, but instead smells of fresh eggs over rice—and he can serve it all year long. (Takashi Ono)

WORKS of JIRO

江戸前のはまぐり
Edo-style *Hamaguri* Clams

はまぐりは江戸前のすし種でも最も古いもののひとつですが、今、東京湾のはまぐりはほとんどありません。30年前、はまぐりは鮨屋のネタから絶滅しかけていて、せいぜい椀種になっているくらいでしたが、次郎が使いました。外国産のはまぐりは固いばかりですが、日本の海で育てると、柔らかなはまぐりになります。
(小野禎一)

Hamaguri clams are one of the oldest Edo-style sushi toppings. But, today, Hamaguri stocks in Tokyo Bay have been depleted. About 30 years ago, these clams nearly disappeared as toppings at sushi restaurants, perhaps only appearing in a soup.

Imported Hamaguri tend to be tough. But when farmed in Japan they become tender. (Yoshikazu Ono)

WORKS of JIRO
香り高いあわび
Fragrant Abalone

昔、あわびはだいたい黒っぽく煮てあって、長く置いてもいいようにしてありました。あわびを塩蒸しにするのも、親父が日本料理店で覚えて、もっと柔らかく鮨に合うように、と工夫してできあがったものです。20年くらい前はあわびも常温で出していたんですが、今はより香りが立つよう、温めて握っています。（小野禎一）

Abalone used to be simmered until quite dark so it would last a long time.
My father is the person who devised the method of salt-steaming abalone, based on techniques gleaned from his work in a Japanese restaurant, to obtain a more tender flesh suited to sushi. 20 years ago he served the abalone at room temperature. Now in order to release its flavor he prepares sushi with slightly warm abalone. (Yoshikazu Ono)

温かいえびの由来
Origin of Warmed Prawn

温かいくるまえびを出すようになったのは、30年ほど前、上野でえびの食中毒があったから。それからちっともえびが出なくなって、どうやったら食べていただけるかと、親父が湯がきたてを常連さんにお出ししたら、これは美味しい、ということで定番になったそうです。今ではどこの鮨屋も温かいえびを出すようになりました。(小野禎一)

 Jiro started parboiling prawns just before preparing them in sushi around 30 years ago, after a bout of food poisoning at a restaurant in Ueno. After that he completely stopped serving prawns. Then my father starting wondering how he could work with the shellfish when he offered a parboiled prawn sushi to a regular customer. When the customer said, "Delicious," it became a signature sushi at Sukiyabashi Jiro. Today, just about every sushi restaurant offers slightly warm prawn sushi. (Yoshikazu Ono)

たまごを焼くまで10年
Ten-year apprenticeship with Eggs

たまごは、次郎のおまかせではフランス料理のデザート。思ったほどたまごは使わず、えびは芝えびを使います。芝えびだけは火を通しても固くならないんです。それにつなぎに大和芋。1時間以上かけて焼き上げます。うちでたまごを焼かせられたらもう一人前ですが、そこに至るまで少なくとも10年はかかります。(小野禎一)

In Sukiyabashi Jiro's tasting menu, our *tamago* course is the equivalent of dessert in French cuisine. That said eggs are used sparingly. We mix in *shiba-ebi* shrimp and *yamatoimo* mountain potato. Even when we heat the shiba-ebi they won't harden. We use the yamatoimo as a binding agent. We carefully grill the egg dish for more than an hour. Once a member of our staff can prepare this dish they are ready to head out on their own. However, mastering our tamago takes about a decade. (Yoshikazu Ono)

鮨の基本は酢めし
Vinegared Rice is at the Heart of Sushi

親父は、「シャリは人肌の温度で」と50年来ずっと言っています。冷たいのとは同じ酢めしと思えないくらい味が違います。米は、普通では炊くのが難しいほど硬い米をよく乾燥してもらい、それを羽釜で炊き上げて、酢の効いたメリハリのあるシャリにします。鮨はあくまで米を食べる食事。すし種も酢めしに合うものだけを使います。(小野禎一)

    For fifty years my father has been saying, "the *shari* rice must be kept at body temperature." If cold, the vinegared rice will have a completely different flavor. At Sukiyabashi Jiro, we use a very hard rice variety that is normally cumbersome to steam. Our supplier also dries it for us for an extended period of time. After steaming, we add considerable vinegar to create our full-bodied sushi rice. Sushi is essentially a rice meal. So we only use toppings that perfectly match our vinegared rice. (Yoshikazu Ono)

WORKS of JIRO

六本木店はより次郎らしく
Essence of Jiro in Roppongi

六本木店では、酢めしは酢を効かせる、藁でかつおをいぶす、こはだやさばは強めに〆る、など本店の親父さんが考え出した次郎ならではのアドバンテージを、より強めに表現しています。一般の方や外国の方にも、『すきやばし次郎』の鮨は、他とここが違いますよ、とより印象的にわかりやすくお伝えしています。(小野隆士)

At the Roppongi branch, I take advantage of the signature styles my father invented by using more vinegar in the rice, more smoking for the *katsuo* (skipjack tuna) and stronger vinegar marinating of *kohada* (gizzard shad) as well as *saba* (mackerel). In this way, I can let our regular guests, and foreign customers, know just how incomparable Jiro's sushi is from the other sushi restaurants. I do it in an dynamic, easy-to-understand way. (Takashi Ono)

準備が95％
It's Mostly in the Preparation

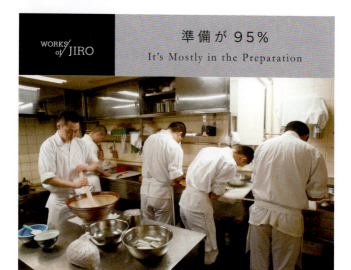

鮨屋は座って注文されたら、すぐに鮨を出します。料理店はお客さまにできるのを待っていただく時間がありますが、鮨屋はあらかじめやっておかないといけません。その準備に時間がかかります。あわびだって4時間くらいかけて仕込んでいますから、準備が9割5分くらい。カウンターでは、もう握るだけです。（小野禎一）

Once you've placed an order in a sushi restaurant the sushi is max right away. That's not true of regular restaurants where diners have to wait a little while for their order to be prepared. In a sushi restaurant, everything has to be arranged in advance. Preparation is time intensive. For instance, we prep the abalone for about four hours. Preparation is about 95 percent of the work. At the counter, our work is simply forming the sushi. (Yoshikazu Ono)

WORKS of JIRO

無言で進む仕事
Working in Silence

仕事中はカウンターの中もシーンとしていますが、お勝手（厨房）も一切言葉がありません。親父さんの手を止めずに一番いい状態で鮨が握れるよう、日頃の仕事の中ですべての段取りができあがっています。親父さんの手に合わせてすべての仕事を進めるから言葉が何もいらない。だから満席でも静かです。
（小野禎一）

    While working there is complete silence, not only behind the counter, but also in the kitchen. No words are exchanged. All the day's prepping procedures are completely in place to allow my father the ability to prepare sushi fluidly under the best possible conditions. Since we've arranged for my father to have everything he requires at hand, there is no need for verbal communication. That's why it's quiet at Sukiyabashi Jiro even when every seat is occupied.
(Yoshikazu Ono)

にぎりは二人三脚
Working in Concert

私が切りつけた魚を親父が握るんですが、お年を召した方や食の細い方には、お客さまの様子を見ながら、ネタの切りつけの厚みや大きさを変えて皿の上で分け、親父の前に並べます。親父は酢めしの量をわからないように変えて、小さめの握りをお出ししています。すると、最後はちょうどいいお腹の具合でお帰りいただけます。（小野禎一）

    I slice the fish. My father prepares the sushi. I will adjust the size and thickness of slices depending on the customer—whether they are elderly or light eaters—and line them up on a plate in front of my father. My father will intuitively adjust the amount of vinegared rice and place a smaller piece in front of the customer. The customer will leave feeling satisfied without being full. (Yoshikazu Ono)

握りも二郎流
Jiro-style *Nigiri*

親父さんの握り方は独特で、酢めしをつかんだ瞬間にもう形ができています。薬指、中指、小指で整えるから握るのが速く、しっかり握っているように見えますが、食べると口の中でハラリと崩れてすし種と一体になります。ゆっくりのときは3拍子、忙しいときは2拍子で握りますが、所作はほとんど変わりません。(小野隆士)

    My father's style of preparing *nigiri* sushi is unique. The moment he has lifted the vinegared rice in his hand he has already created the shape. After using his middle, wedding and pinky digits to gather the rice he quickly drapes a piece of fish over it. It looks like he has applied pressure. Yet when you pop the sushi in your mouth the rice and topping dissolve as one. At a slow pace he makes a nigiri in about three beats and, at a rapid pace, in two beats. But his movements never alter. (Takashi Ono)

仕事道具を磨く
Polishing Work Tools

おひつは毎日磨きます。酢めしを入れる加減か、すぐに黒くなってくるんですね。うちではちょっとでも黒ずんだらやめて、すぐに新しいのを使います。おひつに入れた酢めしが冷めないよう、藁でできた「藁びつ」で保温しますが、藁びつも年に1度は新しいものに替えています。(小野禎一)

We polish our *ohitsu* rice tub everyday. The tubs tend to darken from moisture and vinegar. If our tub shows signs of darkening we will get a new one right away. We place our tub inside an insulating straw basket to keep the sushi rice from going cold. We replace these baskets once every year. (Yoshikazu Ono)

朝晩の掃除
Cleaning twice daily

　鮨屋は清潔でないと、という親父さんの考えから、夜、仕事が終わると、お勝手とカウンター内の調理場にお湯をかけ回して洗い、翌朝の8時には客席の椅子を外に出して、もう一度床を掃除します。土曜日にはカウンターも歯磨き粉で時間をかけて磨きます。だから店内は魚のにおいも酢のにおいもありません。（小野禎一）

　Since my father believes sushi restaurants must be impeccably clean, every night after work we wash down the kitchen and working side of the counter with hot water. The next morning, we place the chairs outside and scrub the floor again. On Saturdays we use polishing powder and take our time to clean the counter. That's why our restaurant never smells of fish nor vinegar. (Yoshikazu Ono)

『すきやばし次郎』の「おまかせ」

　『次郎』の「おまかせコース」は今から15年ほど前にできあがりました。それまでは、ほかの鮨屋同様、お客さまの「お好み」で、注文されたすし種を握っていましたが、懐石料理やフランス料理が、淡い味から濃い味へ、軽快な皿から重厚な皿へという流れを献立に組み込んでいるのを考えて、「鮨」でもやってみようと、まず、白身から握ることを小野二郎が創案しました。いまから、30年前は、どの鮨屋も「おまかせ」と言えば、「まぐろ」から握ったものです。

　コース仕立てにすることで、鮨職人が考える理想的な「その日」の握りが可能になりました。特に、季節のすし種は、仕入れによって毎日順序が入れ替わることがあります。また、かつおの後はしゃこに限る、という名コンビも生まれました。

　これからご案内する「すきやばし次郎の旋律」は、晩春から初秋にかけての「おまかせコース」の一例です。

山本益博

Introduction

Jiro's **omakase** tasting menu was introduced some 15 years ago. Until that time, the chefs made sushi based on the orders of their customers, in the manner of most sushi restaurants. However, when Jiro began contemplating how flavors in **kaiseki** formal multicourse meals and French cuisine moved from light to heavy flavors, as well as light to heavy ingredients, he wanted to apply this menu approach to sushi. First off, he came up with the pioneering idea of starting his tasting menu with a whitefish. If we look back at the *omakase* tasting menu of any sushi restaurant 30 years ago it will have started out with *maguro* tuna.

The implementation of a tasting menu made it possible to achieve a sushi craftsman's ideal: preparing a showcase of that day's finest fish. The tasting menu lineup would also change daily depending on what's in season. Through developing the tasting menu, Jiro made discoveries, such as his famous combination of **shako** (mantis shrimp) following **katsuo** (skipjack tuna).

In the following section, Concerto of Jiro, we will introduce a sample tasting menu from late spring to early summer.

Masuhiro Yamamoto, food critic

Chapter 3

すきやばし次郎の旋律

第1楽章

伝 統

1st Movement   TRADITION

こはだ、まぐろの赤身など「江戸前」の古典的なすし種を中心に、白身の淡い味からまぐろの濃い味へと構成しています。

　　With Edo-style classical sushi ingredients such as *kohada* (gizzard shad) and *maguro* (tuna) at its base, the tasting menu at Sukiyabashi Jiro is composed to slide from the delicate flavor of whitefish to the robust flavor of maguro.

かれい
Karei (Sole)

幕開けのすし種の「かれい」は、淡白な白身。鮨の常識が「最初はまぐろ」だった時代に、淡白な白身を最初に出したのは次郎でした。次郎で初めて食べたほとんどの方は、「お酢が強い」とおっしゃいます。しかし、酢めしの味はこれが江戸前の本筋。食べ進めていくうちに「これでなくては」と納得されるでしょう。

The opening sushi topping, **karei**, is a mild whitefish. Jiro was the first chef to introduce simple whitefish as a menu starter in an era when it was de rigueur in the world of sushi to begin with **maguro**. Most first-time diners at Sukiyabashi Jiro tend to say the sushi rice is heavy on vinegar. But this type of sushi rice represents the authentic Edo-style. As diners continue their meal, they usually come to understand "this is the ultimate sushi rice."

すみいか
Sumi-ika (Golden Cuttlefish)

２貫めは純粋な味わいの「すみいか」。ご覧の通り、丁寧な仕事を施されたいかは、飾りにのりを巻いたり薬味を載せたりはしません。だから美しく、味に一点の曇りもありません。フランス料理の巨匠、ジョエル・ロブションが次郎の鮨を評して、「シンプルを極めるとピュアになる」と言った所以です。

The second piece in the tasting menu is the pure-tasting **sumi-ika**. The beautifully sliced **ika** is not wrapped in a decoration of **nori** or laced with a dressing. That gives it its beauty and completely unadulterated flavor. The maestro of French cuisine Joel Robuchon highly esteems Jiro for the way he demonstrates that, "ultimate simplicity leads to purity."

しまあじ
Shima-aji (Yellow Jack)

３つめの「しまあじ」から次第に力強さが加わってきます。どうですか、口に入れた瞬間にふわっと広がるこの香り。すし種のひとつひとつに固有の香りがあることが、次郎で食べるとよくわかります。また、すし種と酢めしのバランスは天下一品。鮨の理想は扇の地紙の形といわれますが、まさにお手本の姿です。

    From the third piece, **shima-aji**, the flavor becomes more pronounced. The moment you pop it into your mouth the flavor blossoms. Dining at Sukiyabashi Jiro, you become aware of each sushi topping's characteristic aroma. You also taste how the topping variety and sushi rice are always perfectly balanced. Ideally, the topping shape should look like a fan.

あかみ

Akami (Lean Bluefin Tuna)

続いて、まぐろによる３つの変奏曲の始まりです。「あかみ」のヅケの微妙な酸味と鉄分は、醤油との相性が天下一品。とはいえ、生の天然本まぐろでなければ、この味と香りは出せません。このヅケは、食べるときに最高の味になるように人数分を人刻みのタイミングで醤油に漬け込んでいるので、遅刻厳禁です。

    Next up : the start of a trio of **maguro**. In the days before refrigeration, this fish was preserved through marinating in casks of soy sauce in a method called **zuke**. The subtle acidity of the fish and the savory flavor of the soy sauce are a perfect match. This exceptional flavor can only be obtained when using wild tuna. At Sukiyabashi Jiro, we prepare zuke for each of our guests in advance. The preparation is carefully timed. Therefore, we do urge punctuality.

ちゅうとろ
Chutoro (Medium Fatty Bluefin Tuna)

さらに「ちゅうとろ」、「おおとろ」と続いて、風味も次第にクレッシェンドしていきます。豊潤な脂の旨みが口に満ちて、スッと消えて清冽な余韻を残す味わいは圧巻です。先年、アメリカのオバマ大統領が「ちゅうとろ」を召し上がった瞬間、思わずウインクされました。

Now, continuing with **chutoro** (medium fatty tuna) and **otoro** (fatty tuna) we are building up to a crescendo of flavors. The highlight is the way the umami of the rich, fatty flesh blooms in your mouth and disperses immediately, living a clean finish. In 2015, when President Obama dined at Sukiyabashi Jiro, he winked the moment he bit into his piece of chutoro.

おおとろ

Otoro (Fatty Bluefin Tuna)

豊潤なまぐろをいただくと、強い酢めしも「この味でなくては」と納得されるでしょう。口に運んで心地よく舌の上に収まるすし種の寸法は2寸半。これは舌先の長さ、つまり3寸に合わせた寸法で、江戸の頃からの伝統です。口中に味と香りを感じる余白を残しつつほどよく収まる大きさも、美味しさの秘密のひとつです。

When you try this rich **maguro** you'll recognize the reason for the strong vinegared rice. You bring the sushi to your mouth and place it comfortably on your tongue. The length of the topping is around seven centimeters, which is roughly the length of your tongue. It was a tradition of Edo-style sushi from long ago to measure the topping in this way. Creating a size that leaves some space in the mouth to savor the flavor and aroma is one of the secrets of sushi's delectableness.

こはだ
Kohada (Gizzard Shad)

まぐろの後の第１楽章を締めるのは、「こはだ」。小野二郎さんに「いちばん大事なすし種は？」と尋ねると、即座に「こはだ」と答えるほど、江戸前の鮨を代表する握りです。酸味の効いたこはだで口の中をキュッと締めたら、江戸前の伝統を伝える第１楽章から、その時季の選び抜かれたすし種がそろった第２楽章へ。

We follow up **maguro** with **kohada** to conclude the first movement.

If you ask Jiro to name the most important sushi topping the fact he'll immediately respond, "kohada," underscores its place as representative of Edo-style sushi. So, take a bite into this vinegary kohada and let's move onto the second movement where we'll celebrate sushi and the seasons.

第 2 楽章

2nd Movement　THE FOUR SEASONS

その日、築地から仕入れた季節のすし種が最も活きるように順序を考え、調味し、その魚介にふさわしい温度で握ります。

　After procuring the day's seasonal ingredients at Tsukiji, I consider their order of presentation in order to bring out their best qualities. Then I season them and prepare each sushi at its appropriate temperature.

あわび

Awabi (Abalone)

味が転調する第2楽章。まずは、ふくよかに煮上げられた「あわび」。あわびを温かい温度で供した最初が『次郎』ということはあまり知られていませんが、舌触りも香りも生のあわびとは比較になりません。次郎は江戸前のネタを復活させつつ、小野二郎さんが工夫を重ねた新しいすし種を体験できる稀有(けう)な店です。

The second movement features transitions in flavors. Our first piece is richly simmered ***awabi***. Not many people are aware that Jiro was the first to serve abalone warm as sushi. There is no comparing its texture and aroma to raw abalone. Sukiyabashi Jiro is a rare sushi restaurant where you can taste classic Edo-style toppings and also experience Jiro's innovations in sushi.

あじ

Aji (Japanese Horse Mackerel)

次に「あじ」。どこの鮨屋にもある普通のすし種ですが、『次郎』のあじのあまりのすごさに、食べてもあじとわからない人が多々います。築地で普通に仕入れたあじがこんなにみごとな味になるのは、最初の手当が違うため。築地から朝８時に店へ運び、すぐに丁寧な手当をすることで、比類のないネタになります。

Next is **aji**. While this fish is commonly found at sushi restaurants, at Sukiyabashi Jiro its flavor is taken to a whole new level. Some people can't even identify the fish. The aji, which is procured at Tsukiji, gets its rich flavor from intense preparation. After delivery from the market at 8:00 am, the fish is immediately worked on to result in an incomparable sushi topping.

くるまえび
Kuruma-ebi (Japanese Tiger Prawn)

多くの店が「くるまえび」を温かいまま握りますが、30年前に始めたのは次郎です。湯がきたてのえびはほんのり温かく、身の甘みや初めての風味が最大限に引き出されます。みそが先に口に入るように置かれる配慮が「美味しいものを目指すのにこれで終わりということはありません」という次郎の職人魂を表します。

Nowadays, most sushi restaurants serve their **kuruma-ebi** warm, but Jiro was the first to person to do so starting 30 years ago. The parboiled prawn is allowed to slightly cool before being prepared as sushi. The temperature releases the flesh's maximum sweetness and initial flavor. Jiro places the prawn so the customer eats the **miso** (innards) first. This is an expression of Jiro's craftsman spirit, "of constantly pursuing a way to improve on taste."

とりがい

Torigai (Cockle)

続いては繊細な味わいで、春のかそけき味覚の代表、現れたと思ったら2か月も経たないうちに消えてしまう「とりがい」です。ごく軽く湯がいて握られて出てくる姿は、透明な光をまとったように美しく、口に運べば繊細で滋味あふれる美味しさ。こんなに立派なとりがいは最近見ることが減りました。

    The next piece, with its refined flavor, represents late spring. Just when you rejoice that ***torigai*** is in season, two months later and it's gone.

    With light boiling, just before preparing the sushi, the mollusk takes on a beautiful translucent luster. When you place it in your mouth, it has a soft, sweet flavor. These days there are few opportunities to source such fine torigai.

かつお

Katsuo (Skipjack Tuna)

いよいよかつおの出番。初夏から秋にかけての『次郎』のスペシャリテです。かつおは皮目に癖があるので、火であぶって取り除くのですが、強火でやると、うっかりすると焼き魚になってしまいます。そこで、稲藁の柔らかな火であぶると、藁の薫香がついて、口いっぱいにいい香りが広がります。

It's about time for **katsuo**-a Sukiyabashi Jiro specialty from early summer to autumn. Katsuo's skin has a strong flavor, so we remove it through smoking. But if the charcoal is burning too strong the flesh will cook through. By gently smoking over rice straw the katsuo is imparted with a fragrant smokiness, which lingers in your mouth.

しゃこ
Shako (Mantis Shrimp)

続く「しゃこ」は、口中に漂うかつおの余韻を払拭してくれます。しゃこは苦手、とおっしゃる方がいらっしゃいますが、次郎のしゃこには「こんなに美味しいものだったのか」と考えが一変します。ちなみに、上に塗ってあるのは「ツメ」。煮汁を煮詰めて作るからツメと言い、醤油をつけずにそのままいただきます。

Shako works to cleanse the palate from the flavor of the **katsuo**.
Some people say they have an aversion to shako. But after dining at Sukiyabashi Jiro, they often become converts, saying "I didn't know shako could be so good."
Incidentally, the shako is laced with **tsume**. The slightly sweet tsume glaze is made through reduction. Therefore, you do not need to dip your piece into soy sauce.

いわし
Iwashi (Sardine)

夏場の『次郎』のおまかせに欠かせないのが「いわし」です。握られたいわしは妖艶な姿をしています。でも、いつまでも見とれていると、色が変わり、いわしの値打ちがなくなります。ひと目見たら、すぐに召し上がってください。いわしがみるみる溶けていってしまいます。

The summer tasting course at Sukiyabashi Jiro would not be complete without ***iwashi***. Our sardine sushi has a voluptuous silhouette. If you gaze at it for too long, its color changes and its value is lost. After a brief appreciation, please eat it right away. It will melt in your mouth.

さより

Sayori (Halfbeak)

さよりは、冬から春にかけてが旬ですが、季節が随分と延びてきました。以前は、小ぶりのさよりをひねって握っていましたが、今は身の厚い脂の乗ったさよりを握ります。口に運ぶと、滑るような旨みがあり、酢めしとの渾然一体とした感じがたまりません。

Sayori was traditionally in season from winter to spring, but now the season extends for a longer period. We used to twist two thin sayori together to prepare as sushi. Now, we choose a thick, fatty sayori. When you place it in your mouth there's an umami that glides on your tongue and a pleasing harmony as the topping and the vinegared rice become one.

第3楽章

進化

3rd Movement   EVOLUTION

「江戸前」の鮨が進化した軍艦巻きを並べ、『次郎』の名物
あなごとたまごで「おまかせ」コースのフィナーレを飾ります。

Alongside the *gunkan-maki* (literally "battleship roll") that
advanced Edo-style sushi, Jiro's famous *anago* (conger) and
tamago (eggs) mark the finale of the omakase tasting menu.

うに
Uni (Sea Urchin)

いよいよフィナーレの第3楽章。その幕開けは、3貫続く軍艦巻きです。まずはジョエル・ロブションが「まるでクリーム」と評した「うに」。この最上級のうには、今や貴重品です。そんなうにに匹敵する味の立役者がのり。毎朝、備長炭の火で丹念にあぶったのりの豊かな風味と、濃厚なうにとさらに酢めしとの三重奏の趣です。

And now we reach the finale with the third movement. We open with three fish varieties served as **gunkan-maki.** First, our **uni**, which Joel Robuchon exclaimed, "was like eating cream." The class of uni we serve is now hard to come by, and is considered precious. Nori is used to enhance this paragon of flavor. The nori, which is toasted every morning over fine **binchotan** charcoal, is married with the rich, complex flavor of the uni along with the vinegared rice, becoming one. It's a trio of delightful flavors.

こばしら

Kobashira (Mactra Clam Muscle)

続く「こばしら」は、名前に反して実に大きな粒ぞろい。さっぱりとして小味の効いた、香りの良い一品です。このサイズのこばしらも、もうほとんど河岸(かし)にも出ないそう。今のうちに、しかと覚えておきたい味わいです。小野二郎さん曰く、「あと30年も経てば、今のおまかせの流れは、できなくなってるでしょう」。

    This next piece has an appearance contrary to what its name means in Japanese (small bridge), as it is actually an enormous muscle. It makes for a wonderful sushi with its fine aroma and refreshing, subtle flavor. These days you rarely find such large muscles at the market. Be sure to savor this muscle in the near future. According Jiro Ono, "In about 30 years, we will no longer be able to include this muscle in our tasting menu."

いくら

Ikura (Salmon Roe)

3貫めの「いくら」は、次郎で唯一の冷凍もの。ただし、最も美味しい時期に、新鮮な風味を保って冷凍した次郎の自家製で、そのあまりの自然な美味しさにほとんどの人は冷凍ものとは気づきません。何年もの試行錯誤の末、年中出せるようになったその風味は、魚卵と言うより卵かけごはんのように濃厚です。

Our third battleship roll is made with *ikura*, the only fish that Jiro freezes.
That said, he procures the finest, seasonal ikura and prepares it according to his special house method. The flavor is so naturally tasty that most diners have no idea it has been frozen. The flavor of his ikura, which can be served throughout the year, was achieved through experimentation. Many people say It has a rich flavor like a raw egg over rice rather than salmon roe."

あなご
Anago (Conger Eel)

続いて「あなご」の登場です。次郎のあなごは、煮上げた時点で最高の味。後であぶったりしません。口に入れると即座に消え去るあなごは、二郎さんが中指、薬指、小指を巧みに使い、酢めしに空気を含ませながら握ります。その独特の握り方で生まれる口当たりは軽く、置いた瞬間に、鮨がわずかに沈むほどです。

At Jiro, our **anago** is perfectly finished when it is simmered.

We do not broil it later when preparing sushi. Jiro uses his middle, ring and pinky fingers to pump air into the vinagered rice as he shapes the anago sushi. It is so tender and light it melts right away in your mouth. Jiro creates a sushi that is airy in the mouth and once on your tongue seems to immediately dissolve.

たまご

Tamago (Grilled Eggs)

締めくくりの「たまご」は、昔は握りで出していました。現在は数多くの握りの後なので、そのまま。ムラなく美しいきつね色に焼き上げたたまごを頬張れば、しっとりとした口当たりの後にやさしい甘みがじんわりと広がります。だし巻き卵とは違う、江戸前の鮨屋のデザートです。

Tamago, which is the final offering in our omakase tasting menu, used to be prepared as sushi. Nowadays, since it follows many sushi pieces, the egg is served alone. When you bite into the tamago, which is grilled to an even golden brown, you first notice the firm texture. This is gradually followed by a gentle, sweet flavor that blooms in your mouth. Unlike the **dashimaki tamago** (rolled omelet with dashi stock), this could qualify as dessert at an Edo-style sushi restaurant.

ジョエル・ロブション
Joel Robuchon

フランス料理界の巨匠、ヨーロッパ、アメリカ、アジア各地に自分の名を冠した店を持つ。

『すきやばし次郎』さんへ

1986年から30年通い続けています。
ムッシュー・ジローの鮨は、常に酢めしと魚に敬意を払い、シンプルにして、奥行きが深く、味わいはピュアです。
しかも、90歳になられても、通うたびに酢めしなどが進化しているのは、驚くべきこと!
店内は魚の匂いもなんの匂いもなく、清潔感も比類ありません。魚介の質の高さ、包丁技術などの仕事も抜きんでていて、「JIRO」は世界最高の1軒です。

" Homage to Jiro

I have been visiting Sukiyabashi Jiro since 1986.
Monsieur Jiro's sushi always holds vinegared rice and fish in the highest regard. His sushi is simple, shows depth and its flavor is pure. Even though he is 90 years old, every time I drop in I notice he has made some improvement on the vinegared rice and other things. It is amazing!
There is no odor of fish, no odor at all in the restaurant. It is the cleanest restaurant ever. The fish quality and knife work, as well as other techniques, are all of the highest order…All these make Jiro one of the best restaurants in the world. "

マッシモ・ボットゥーラ
Massimo Bottura

2016年度、世界ベスト50レストランの第1位に輝く、イタリア「オステリア・フランチェスカーナ」オーナーシェフ。

『すきやばし次郎』さんへ

地下鉄の階段を降りて味覚の楽園へ。そこは二郎さん親子が「日々に埋もれない日々」を生きる空間です。
お二人が技を極め、自らの器を知り、舌を養い、己を探究してきた店。そうした空間・瞬間に息づく職人の取り組みは、実に知的なものです。食材、技術、知識、そして何より、品質へのこだわり。そのすべてを駆使した挑戦がそこにはあるのです。
ここでは一口サイズの「噛める文化」にすべてが凝縮されています。
情熱の味わいから私たちにもたらされるもの。それは感動です。

" Homage to Jiro

Descending the stairs into a paradise of taste sensations.
There, a space where father and son spend *"days without being buried by the days."*
It's a restaurant where the pair has explored the mastering of techniques, the filling of vessels with knowledge, the nourishing of the tongue. The dedicated work of the craftsmen living in the space, in the moment, is in fact an intellectual thing. Ingredients, technique, knowledge and, more than anything, a devotion to quality… Here, the challenge is to utilize them all.
These elements are all condensed in this single-bite culture. The flavor of passion is served to us. And this is deeply moving. "

お知らせ　Information

『すきやばし次郎』は、観光名所ではありません。季節が違えば、夏なら「かつお」「あわび」冬なら「さば」「たこ」といった具合にすし種が変わります。一度訪れて気に入られたら、ぜひ、違う季節にいらしてみてください。訪れるたびに、『すきやばし次郎』の良さに気づいていただけるはずです。

Dining at Sukibayashi Jiro is not like visiting a tourist attraction. Different seasons bring different sushi, for example **katsuo** (skipjack tuna) and **awabi**(Abalone) in summer, and saba (mackerel) and **tako** (octopus) in winter. If you have enjoyed your experience at Sukiyabashi Jiro, be sure to come again. Each visit will bring new discoveries.

すきやばし次郎
住所：東京都中央区銀座 4-2-15　塚本素山ビル B1
電話：03-3535-3600　営業時間：11:30-14:00,17:30-20:30
（土曜日は昼のみ営業）定休日：土曜夜　日曜、祝日
Sukiyabashi Jiro
Address : Tsukamoto-sozan Building B1, 4-2-15 Ginza Chuo-ku Tokyo
Phone : 03-3535-3600
Open : 11:30 am to 2:00 pm; 5:30 pm to 8:30 pm on weekdays and 11:30 am to 2:00 pm on Saturdays. **Closed :** Sundays and holidays

---

すきやばし次郎　六本木店
住所：東京都港区六本木 6-12-2
電話：03-5413-6626　営業時間：11:30-14:00、17:30-21:00
定休日：水曜日
Sukiyabashi Jiro -Roppongi
Address : 6-12-2 Roppongi, Minato-ku, Tokyo
Phone : 03-5413-6626
Open : 11:30 am to 2:00 pm; 5:30 pm to 9 pm on weekdays and Sundays
Closed : Wednesdays

小野二郎（おの・じろう） 1925年（大正14年）静岡県、現・浜松市生まれ。8歳で地元の料理旅館に奉公に出て、13歳のころには結婚式の仕出し料理をひとりで作るほどの腕になった。16歳で軍需工場、19歳で軍隊に入り、終戦後、26歳の時に東京・京橋の名店『与志乃』で鮨職人に。1965年に独立し、以来50年以上、鮨を握り続けている。「現代の名工」であり、黄綬褒章受勲。

Jiro Ono   Born in 1925 in present-day Hamamatsu, Shizuoka Prefecture. At the age of eight, he became an apprentice at a local restaurant-inn. He was so skilled that by the time he was 13 he was in charge of creating the cuisine for wedding banquets. At 16 he was sent to work at a munitions factory and at 19 joined the military. Following the war, he became a sushi craftsman at the famous Yoshino restaurant in Kyobashi, Tokyo. He was 26. In 1965, he struck out on his own, and, for over 50 years, has been preparing sushi. He was awarded Japan's prestigious Medal with Yellow Ribbon for dedication to his profession.

小野禎一（おの・よしかず） 1959年（昭和34年）大阪府天王寺区生まれ。高校卒業後、父・二郎氏の勧めで東京・赤坂の日本料理店『大友』などで料理の基礎を学び、1983年より『すきやばし次郎』で仕入れと仕込みを任される。『大友』と『次郎』のふたりの師匠は、そろって優れた技術を持つ職人の証「現代の名工」である。現在は『すきやばし次郎』店主。

Yoshikazu Ono   Born in 1959 in Osaka Prefecture. Following high school, Yoshikazu went to work at Otomo restaurant in Akasaka on the recommendation of his father, in order to study the fundamentals of Japanese cuisine. From 1983, he joined Sukiyabashi Jiro and took charge of procuring and prepping supplies. Having gained experience under two culinary giants, Otomo and Jiro, Yoshikazu was recognized by the goverment for his master techniques. Today, he is the head of Sukiyabashi Jiro.

小野隆士（おの・たかし） 1961年（昭和36年）静岡県浜松市生まれ。幼少のころから物を作るのが好きで、8歳で鮨職人を志す。高校卒業後、『すきやばし次郎』の本店と『すきやばし次郎日本橋高島屋店』に勤務し、『すきやばし次郎』で23年間腕を磨いた後、2003年から六本木店の親方になる。鮨の食べ方の丁寧な説明は、外国の方にも好評。

Takashi Ono   Born in 1961 in Hamamatsu, Shizuoka Prefecture.
From a young age, Takashi enjoyed working with his hands. At the age of eight, he was determined to become a sushi craftsman. Following high school, Takashi began working at Sukiyabashi Jiro as well as its annex in the Takashimaya Nihonbashi store. After honing his skills at Jiro for 23 years, Takashi became the head chef of Jiro's Roppongi branch in 2003. He is known for his easy-to-understand explanations on all matters related to sushi and sushi etiquette to his customers from overseas.

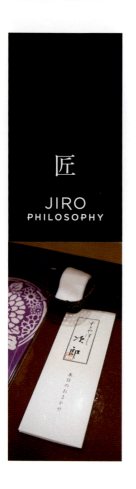

匠　すきやばし次郎　JIRO PHILOSOPHY

著者：	小野二郎、山本益博
撮影：	泉　健太
取材：	高島英治
翻訳：	Noriko Norica-Panayota Kitano Kate Klippensteen
デザイン：	宮坂　淳
編集：	尾崎　靖（小学館）

プリンティング・ディレクション：
　　　　　野口啓一（TOPPAN株式会社）

協力：　すきやばし次郎、フジタ水産、
　　　　司水産、水栄、八百金、手源、
　　　　大秋、泉千、渡辺、熊梅、
　　　　三谷栄亮商店、朝日園

2016年7月30日　　第１版第１刷発行
2025年5月17日　　　　第4刷発行

著作者：	小野二郎、山本益博、 小野禎一、小野隆士
発行者：	宮澤明洋
発行所：	株式会社 小学館 東京都千代田区一ツ橋2-3-1 〒101-8001 **編集：** 03-3230-5707 **販売：** 03-5281-3555
印刷所：	TOPPANクロレ株式会社
製本所：	牧製本印刷株式会社

造本には十分注意しておりますが、印刷、製本などの製造上の不備がございましたら「制作局コールセンター」（フリーダイヤル0120-336-340）にご連絡ください。電話受付は、土・日・祝休日を除く9:30〜17:30。本書の無断での複写（コピー）、上演、放送等の二次利用、翻案等は、著作権法上の例外を除き禁じられています。本書の電子データ化などの無断複製は、著作権法上の例外を除き、禁じられています。代行業者等の第三者による電子的複製も認められておりません。

© JIRO ONO, MASUHIRO YAMAMOTO, YOSHIKAZU ONO, TAKASHI ONO , 2016 .
Printed in JAPAN. ISBN978-4-09-388497-6